The Rain Forest

Protecting the Rain Forest

Mae Woods
ABDO Publishing Company

visit us at
www.abdopub.com

Published by Abdo Publishing Company 4940 Viking Drive, Edina, Minnesota 55435.
Copyright © 1999 by Abdo Consulting Group, Inc. International copyrights reserved in all
countries. No part of this book may be reproduced in any form without written permission
from the publisher.

Printed in the United States.

Photo credits: Peter Arnold, Inc., AP/Wide World

Edited by Lori Kinstad Pupeza
Contributing editor Morgan Hughes
Graphics by Linda O'Leary

Library of Congress Cataloging-in-Publication Data

Woods, Mae.
          Protecting the rain forest / Mae Woods.
          p. cm. -- (The rain forest)
          Includes index.
          Summary: Describes the characteristics of rain forests, their importance to the
          world's environment, and what can be done to preserve them from further
          destruction.
          ISBN 1-57765-022-0
          1. Rain forest conservation--Juvenile literature. 2. Rain forest ecology--Juvenile
          literature. [1. Rain forest conservation. 2. Rain forest ecology. 3. Ecology.] I. Title.
          II. Series: Woods, Mae. Rain forest.
          SD411.W66   1999
          333.75'16'0913--dc21   98-13432
                                                                      CIP
                                                                      AC

Note to reader
The words in the text that are the color green refer to the words in the glossary.

Contents

The Rain Forest 4

Weather Control 6

Endangered Animals 8

Protecting the Trees.......................... 10

Chico Mendes.................................... 12

Forest Reserves 14

Mining and Farming 16

The Future 18

A World View 20

Glossary 22

Internet Sites 23

Index 24

The Rain Forest

*T*he world continues to discover new riches in the rain forests. Recently, a new species of marmoset monkeys was found in the Amazon. It is the size of a mouse. At the same time that findings like this are being made, some species of plants and animals are in danger of disappearing. They could become extinct without ever having been discovered.

Half of the world's tropical forests have already been destroyed. The jungles are being cleared away by loggers, miners, farmers, cattle ranchers, and builders. These groups may not understand the results of cutting down the trees. Without the food and shelter of the tall trees, many animals will die.

Tropical countries are taking steps to protect their rain forests. They are setting aside land as parks and reserves. They are making new products they can sell. They are learning that their lush forests have many unique things to offer the rest of the world.

Many of the world's tropical forests have been destroyed.
This rain forest has been cleared to build the Brazil-Trans Amazon highway.

Weather Control

*R*ain forests receive half of the rain that falls on the earth. Trees and plants help recycle the rain. They absorb most of the water then release the moisture back into the air. The moisture forms clouds that move around and rain on other places. There would be less rainfall everywhere if there were fewer trees in the rain forests.

Trees also release oxygen into the air. When automobiles burn fuel, a gas called carbon dioxide is produced. Green plants absorb carbon dioxide, and release fresh oxygen. If there aren't enough plants in the world, carbon dioxide forms an invisible shield around the earth that traps the heat of the sun, like in a glass greenhouse. This is called the greenhouse effect. Because of this, the planet may become a few degrees warmer. It may soon become too hot to grow certain crops.

Protecting the rain forest trees will help control the weather and prevent global warming.

Natural Cycle

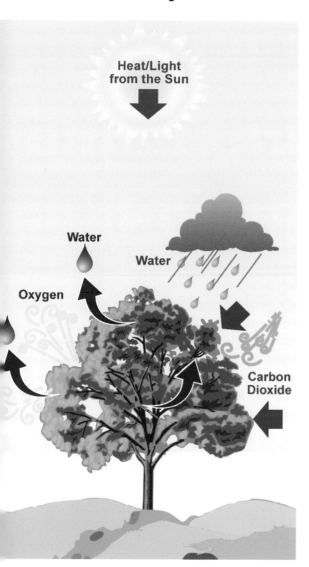

Heat/Light from the Sun

Water

Water

Oxygen

Carbon Dioxide

Greenhouse Effect

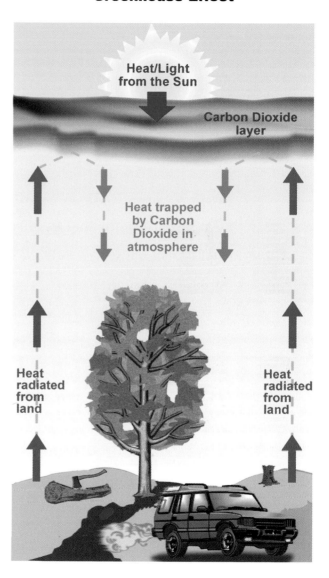

Heat/Light from the Sun

Carbon Dioxide layer

Heat trapped by Carbon Dioxide in atmosphere

Heat radiated from land

Heat radiated from land

KEY ▮ Taken in by plants   ▮ Given off by plants

Endangered Animals

When the rain forest trees are cut down, millions of insects, birds, and other animals lose their homes. They also lose their sources of food. They can move to new areas, but they will have to compete with other groups of animals to stay alive. Many will die.

There are only one hundred golden tamarin monkeys left in the world. This unique animal is one of many creatures who have become endangered species. Without help, it may become extinct.

Today, a zoo is raising baby tamarins and teaching them how to live in the wild. The adult tamarins will be returned to jungles. Many endangered animals, such as the indiri lemur, will not survive in cages. The people of Madagascar have created a special reserve so the lemurs can live in their natural environment.

Pictured is a tamarin monkey. Other endangered animals include the orangutan, mountain gorilla, tiger, Malaysian tapir, Malaysian elephant, and the rhinoceros of Sumatra.

Protecting the Trees

Many types of hardwood come from rain forest trees. Mahogany, rosewood, and teak are beautiful woods used to build furniture and boats. Lumber has been the rain forest's most valuable export.

However, cutting down the trees disturbs animal and plant life. It also affects the weather and the soil. Without the trees, the topsoil washes away. When it rains, the soil runs down to the river and forms blocks of mud. The river cannot move because of all the mud, so the water rises and floods the land.

Logging has already hurt huge areas of the rain forests. People are learning that they must limit the number of trees that can be removed. They must also find ways of logging that does not hurt the environment. Now, some loggers only remove trees from small areas and leave circles of jungle around each clearing. New trees and plants soon grow in the logged areas.

**This child is standing in front of a tree that was cut down
in an African rain forest.**

Chico Mendes

Chico Mendes was born and raised in the Brazilian rain forest. His father and brothers worked as rubber tappers. When he grew up, he joined them collecting latex from rubber trees. In 1969, a highway was built through the forest. Settlers moved in and began to clear away the trees so they could raise cattle. Rubber tappers were forced to leave their homes and find other places to work.

Chico Mendes refused to leave. He spoke out against the destruction of the rain forest. Mendes convinced the government of Brazil to set aside a large region of land as a forest reserve. Here, the trees would be protected.

Many local ranchers fought against Mendes and the other rubber tappers. In 1988, Chico Mendes was killed by one of his enemies. His courage has inspired many people to carry on his mission to protect the rain forests.

Brazil

Atlantic Ocean

Chico Mendes fought to preserve the Brazilian rain forest.

Forest Reserves

Many countries have set aside areas of rain forests as reserves or national parks. Plants and wildlife thrive in these protected areas. Visitors like to come and watch animals in their natural settings.

A reserve in Madagascar provides a safe home for 12 different types of lemurs. A park in Malaysia protects 3,000 species of butterflies. Many kinds of rare birds live in Manu National Park in Peru and Tortuguero National Park in Costa Rica. Korup National Park in western Africa is a good model for new reserves.

Korup National Park has a special area called a core, surrounded by two buffer zones. The core is protected. Hunting, logging, and farming are not allowed. In the first buffer zone, natives can harvest wild plants. It is also open to tourists and scientists. In the next zone, local people can farm, gather wood, and raise animals for hunting.

A butterfly in a Costa Rican rain forest.

Mining and Farming

Precious minerals such as gold, silver, and copper have been found in rain forests. When gold was discovered in the Amazon, a large area of the jungle was destroyed to build a mine. Miners used mercury to separate the gold from the ore. The mercury washed into the river and poisoned the fish. Natives who ate the fish became sick.

When people saw the damage that was being done, they began to seek new ways of mining. They have stopped using mercury. People are also finding better ways to farm. In the past, farmers would burn down large areas and use the ash to grow new crops. After two years the soil lost all its nutrients and nothing would grow.

Natives have learned to farm in smaller areas and to let the land grow wild for several years before planting again. This allows the soil to recover.

The Carajas iron mine in what was part of a Brazilian rain forest.

The Future

*T*he world sees the need to protect rain forests from further destruction. Logging can be done with more care. Lost trees can be replaced with new growth. People living in rain forests also know they can develop other products to sell so that wood is not their main export. Sweet smelling oils from plants are being sold for use in soap and shampoo. Unusual fruits and cooking oils made from palm and bananas are being exported.

New discoveries are being made. Scientists found that the sap from trees in Brazil makes a fuel that can be used to heat homes. Nuts from trees in the Philippines are another amazing new source of fuel. The oil from petroleum nuts is

flammable. For many years, natives have burned it in oil lamps. Six trees can grow enough nuts to light a family's home for one year. Can you imagine dining by nut light?

The Kilimanjaro rain forest in Tanzania, Africa.

A World View

*R*ain forests cover a very small area of the globe, but they are important to everyone in the world. Rain forests help to provide clean air. They recycle rain to cool the planet. They have given food, spices, medicine, and many valuable products to the world. They are home to many kinds of the plants and animals on the earth. The rain forests must be kept healthy.

People support the preservation of rain forests in many different ways. They visit forest reserves and buy native products that have been developed as renewable resources. They learn about the governments of countries with rain forests. They join groups that provide information about these special places and their needs. They urge their own leaders to offer aid to countries with rain forests.

Everyone can do something to help preserve the riches of the rain forests and protect them from harm.

Tree ferns in a Caribbean rain forest.

Glossary

Absorb - to soak up or take in.

Affects - has an effect on; changes.

Buffer zone - the area surrounding the core in a forest reserve.

Cultivate (kul-TEE-vate) - to prepare and use for growing crops; to help to grow.

Destruction (d-STRUK-shun) - being ruined or torn down.

Endangered species - a group of animals or plants in danger of becoming extinct.

Environment (n-vi-ROE-ment) - all the things that surround a person, animal, or plant and affect its well-being.

Export - to send from one country to another.

Extinct - no longer in existence anywhere in the world.

Flammable - easily set on fire.

Global warming - the increase in heat on the surface of the earth.

Greenhouse effect - the warm effect produced when heat from the sun is trapped close to the earth.

Latex - a milky, white substance that can be made into rubber.

Model - a good example that ought to be copied; a style or design.

Nutrients (new-TREE-ents) - food that plants and animals need in order to grow.

Oxygen - a gas that has no color, taste, or smell, found in air and water.

Preservation - the act of protecting from harm; kept in a certain condition.

Recycle - to put something through a special process so it can be used again.

Renewable resource - a useful product or thing that can be made again.

Sap - liquid that flows through a tree or plant.

Species (SPEE-sheez) - a group of plants or animals that are alike in certain ways.

Tourists - travelers; visitors.

Internet Sites

Amazon Interactive
http://www.eduweb.com/amazon.html
Explore the geography of the Ecuadorian rain forest through on-line games and activities. Discover the ways that the Quichua live off the land. Then try your hand at running a community-based ecotourism project along the Río Napo.

Living Edens: Manu, Peru's Hidden Rain Forest
http://www.pbs.org/edens/manu/
This site is about the animals and indigenous people who populate Peru's Manu region.

The Rain Forest Workshop
http://kids.osd.wcdnct.edu/Marshall/rainforest_home_page.html
The Rain Forest Workshop was developed by Virginia Reid and the students at Thurgood Marshall Middle School, in Olympia, Washington. This site is one of the best school sites around with links to many other sites as well as great information on the rainforest.

The Tropical Rain Forest in Suriname
http://www.euronet.nl/users/mbleeker/suriname/suri-eng.html
A multimedia tour through the rain forest in Suriname (SA). Read about plants, animals, Indians, and Maroons. This site is very organized and full of information.

These sites are subject to change. Go to your favorite search engine and type in Rain Forest for more sites.

Pass It On

Rain Forest Enthusiasts: educate readers around the country by passing on information you've learned about rain forests. Share your little-known facts and interesting stories. Tell others about animals, insects, or people of the rain forest. We want to hear from you!

To get posted on the ABDO Publishing Company website E-mail us at
"Science@abdopub.com"

Visit the ABDO Publishing Company website at www.abdopub.com

Index

A

Africa 14
Amazon 4, 16
animals 4, 8, 14, 20
automobiles 6

B

birds 8, 14
Brazil 12, 18

C

carbon dioxide 6
crops 6, 16

D

destruction 12, 18

E

environment 8, 10
export 10, 18
extinct 4, 8

F

farmers 4, 16
floods 10
forest reserve 12, 20
fuel 6, 18

G

global warming 6
gold 16
greenhouse effect 6

I

insects 8

J

jungles 4

L

loggers 4, 10
lumber 10

M

Madagascar 8, 14
Malaysia 9, 14
marmoset 4
medicine 20
Mendes, Chico 12
mercury 16
miners 4, 16

N

national parks 14
natives 14, 18

O

oxygen 6

P

plants 4, 6, 10, 14,
    18, 20
preservation 20
products 4, 18, 20

R

rainfall 6
ranchers 4, 12
recycle 6, 20
river 10, 16
rubber 12

S

scientists 14, 18
soil 10, 16
species 4, 14

T

tiger 9
trees 4, 6, 8, 10, 12,
    18
tropical 4

W

weather 6, 10